CROSSINGS

poems by

Kathryn Kimball

Finishing Line Press
Georgetown, Kentucky

CROSSINGS

Copyright © 2021 by Kathryn Kimball
ISBN 978-1-64662-610-6 First Edition
All rights reserved under International and Pan-American Copyright Conventions. No part of this book may be reproduced in any manner whatsoever without written permission from the publisher, except in the case of brief quotations embodied in critical articles and reviews.

ACKNOWLEDGMENTS

For their steadfast encouragement, I thank my family, friends, poets of the UWS Poetry Group, of the Gatehouse, and on the Moving Walkway. Deep gratitude to my mentors at Drew University and also to my husband, Andrew, for unfailing support and love.

Quotation on page 29 with author's permission
Guy Goffette, "L'ordalie," Pain perdu, Gallimard, 2020

Publisher: Leah Huete de Maines
Editor: Christen Kincaid
Cover Art: Sisters Meta and Mae (Biz) Chesser, studio portrait, North Alabama, c. 1915
Author Photo: Ceinwen McMillan
Cover Design: Elizabeth Maines McCleavy

Order online: www.finishinglinepress.com
also available on amazon.com

Author inquiries and mail orders:
Finishing Line Press
PO Box 1626
Georgetown, Kentucky 40324
USA

Table of Contents

Photographer's Studio, 1915 1

Southern Banshee 2

Bingo 1958 3

Nothing Is Odd 4

Potato Picking in Baldwin County, 1938 5

Wedding Day, March 1945 6

Peeling Peaches 7

Scepter for My Mother 8

Daddy Shaving 9

Gold Ring 10

Having Words 11

My Daughter Is Transfigured 12

Wedding Picture 13

A Tale 15

Our Happiness 16

Love Poem for My Husband 17

Jung Potatoes 18

I Thought I Knew It All 20

A Blessing 21

West Seventy-Sixth St. 22

& 25

Palimpsest 26

Crossings 27

The Simple Heart of Things 29

A Dream 30

Leaves Falling in Late October 31

For my family, near and far, always close

Photographer's Studio, 1915

In makeshift light,
in the faux furnishing
of rattan chair and painted garden,
I see two sisters posed for eternity.

One is sun, trusting;
one is moon, waning:
Cherished kin before me,
where is my grave?

In the pristine lace of my dress,
says Sun.
In the dark folds of my skirt,
says Moon.

I, who am making
my crossing
of years,
reply:

I know your light,
your dark,
that this moment is lit
in a flash.

Yet, hold me
still.
I am not posed
for eternity.

Southern Banshee

She sits on a threadbare sofa.
Across the lap of her house-dress
she cradles a steel-string guitar
bought on layaway for $2 a month.

In the high-wailing voice
of a Southern banshee
she begins to strum and sing:
"Now folks I'll tell a story…"

My brother and I sit, acolytes,
at her barefooted feet
her toes and fingers flecked
with old polish

her wild black-dyed hair
barely restrained with pins
her nose crooked from a husband's mean fist
her mouth creased with snuff.

She's our TV star
an unknown diva from a gypsy caravan
a comet out of nowhere, blazing
within the housing project's walls.

Bingo 1958
>*Masonic Temple, 1021 Madison Avenue*
>*Montgomery, Alabama*

Every Tuesday brought Bingo to the Temple.
My grandma's money sources were never ample:
Social Security from working at the mill
And whatever my mother could afford to give.
Just some dollars tucked along with hope
In a tiny pouch for change, its clasp
Of brassy heads twisted in a kiss
And secreted in her patent leather purse.
"Ya'll be good," she said, and we were left
To watch the common room's TV set
While she took the stairs to Bingo heaven.
Then on a drink-stained carpet we stretched prone –
My brother and I – breathing leftover smoke
From old Masonic lungs this side of dank.
We were in our heaven too. Never
Had we had the luxury of this fever
Called TV, by Mama: "Idiot Box."
In stupor we watched the shows sure to shock
In those rumbling times – *Peter Gunn,*
Have Gun Will Travel, Gun Smoke, Rifleman.
Even the show's sponsoring golden calf
Offered a catching jingle or a laugh.
We never understood very much
Of this black and white universe.
But if, at Bingo's end, she coined the slot
To call a cab, we knew she'd won the pot.
Otherwise, we'd trudge like grumbling soldiers
The two miles home, Grandma's self-composure
As faultless as a queen's. She'd learned to guard
Her secrets close, like a hand of cards –
Lessons learned when a husband's fist
Came from nowhere to her face. The fist
Hit square, Mama revealed to me the last
Week of her life, unburdening her past:
"Your grandma always stood her ground; I've seen
Her hold a burning lamp of kerosene
And take a blow." She spoke to me from dark
Recesses of a lady's pocketbook.

Nothing is Odd

Mother says when she was young and poor
five of them slept crosswise in a bed
like sardines in a pop-top tin of oil.
Even the patchwork quilts did not resist
tucked as they were under the mattress side.
Mother says nothing is ever odd
when nothing is what everybody has.

Potato Picking in Baldwin County, 1938

The week before my mother died
she wanted to remember being twelve
working the fields in South Alabama
with her older brother Talmadge
picking potatoes sun up to sun down
picking up rows and rows
of dirty potatoes swollen with starch
10 cents an hour for a 12-hour day
with the bonus of carrying home
the culls otherwise thrown to the pigs
all the earnings given to Mama
who gave them 15 cents to spend
perhaps for a drink or a Milky Way
maybe even a matinee.

Nothing could be more revolting
to a twelve-year-old she said
than sticking your fingers deep into
a stinking ripe rotten potato
and nothing more rewarding than
completing a row before the mules
had finished digging up the next
so brother and sister could relax
in the shadow of the end row oak
with an ice-cold Nehi grape
kept frosty in a tub of ice
bought with a hard-earned nickel plus
a sweaty-flushed face, then chugalugged down
while shaded from the white-hot sun.

Wedding Day, March 1945

They pose in front of the flowering azalea
my father standing as straight as he can despite
the kyphosis from a fall down an Alaskan ice hill during the war
the black and white of the photo giving his suit a crisp definition—
the sharpness of desire;

my mother, her stylish hat round, perched on the front
of her head like the "dough-nut" it was called, back then
when people wanted the everyday glazed, made buoyant;
her shoes, two-toned, two leathers sewn seamlessly into one,
her dark slim dress trimmed in white.

both wanting solid ground underfoot,
he ten years older than his bride, farm-boy with dreams to be more
because of her, only eighteen, who had vowed
never again to dig for potatoes.

Wanda, you will think of divorce within the year, learn
his handsome face and solid gait
are not a match for your ardent mind, given to adventure and outburst.
I've heard you say it —
"I married the wrong man but got the right children."
Seventeen years later, you, hurting, said, "It's over."
Years after that, you, forgiving, declared, "He was good in bed."

Peeling Peaches

Late August sun
bakes the stucco house
while I peel peaches, waiting
for your Chevy to crunch the gravel.

The long drive in Alabama heat
hasn't wilted your blue shirt.
Is it for me or Mama
that you look as cool as beer

straight as a fishing rod?
It's just me peeling peaches
in the old yellow kitchen.
You tighten the dripping faucet,

put on an apron, sit down to help,
your Army-cook fingers, which are mine,
make the sweet plump balls in the basket
disappear. One more Saturday visit

dreaded, with Mama making sure
she's not around to hear about new wife
Horse Face; I will live to see them friends,
Daddy, and you, a ghost,

a friend to me, peeling peaches,
listening to the faucet drip.

Scepter for My Mother

How I loved your cylinders of gold
sheltering thin columns of red,
the tint of winter berries, soft-scented
as a sweet-pea, smooth as the lips
which called for it. How ingeniously
they turned into spiraling obelisks,
with just a twist of the fingers.

Even Cleopatra's lip-stain
of crushed beetle and ant egg,
its bright carmine guarded
in jars of smooth alabaster,
could not cause the wonder
of your Revlon Indelible-Crème,
your New-and-Forever Red.

I watched from my groundling seat
as you, poised on the vanity stool,
compact mirror in hand, spun out
the crimson finger of soft paint, then glossed
your lips. How they took the color—Cupid's bow
deftly drawn, lower lip smoothed in double-time,
then the sweet excess transferred to tissue
with one neat blot. You lived with verve.

You nearly died without it. In the hospital,
intubated, wan, heavily drugged to keep you
from expressive speech, you signaled
for your tube of power. Around your mouth's
tracheal hose, I dabbed Royal Red—
vamp magic to restore you
to one more year of life.

Daddy Shaving

When he wasn't looking,
I would hold the razor's
slender handle

feel its roughened grip
swirl the brush's stiff bristles
into the mug of hard soap
make myself a fragrant foam.

I had watched him often enough—
whisking the brush in the mug
stirring in hot rivulets of water

spreading the lather in small circles
on his face and neck.
mowing away soap and whiskers
in dexterous swathes.

He never forgot a splash of Old Spice,
and when he was done, it felt good
to kiss his smooth, sweet-smelling cheek.

When he was ninety, forgetful, bed-ridden,
I bought him Old Spice,
thinking he might like the sight,
the smell of his old after-shave.

The creamy-beige ceramic bottle
with its blue sailboat
and tiny metal cap

sat on his bedside table
untouched.
I kissed
a whiskery face.

Gold Ring

I felt the vine of thought reaching into shadows.
its tendrils groping at nothing.
I was six, sitting by you on the slip-covered sofa,
watching your eyes travel the newspaper.
The newsprint ran together like magnetized shavings.

"Will I die?
You folded the newspaper.
Without hesitating, you removed the gold ring from your finger.
"You are like this ring. No beginning and no end."

For the twenty years since your death
I have worn that ring,
believed your golden,
defiant annulus,
nulling poles, logic,
even words.

Having Words
    for my mother

I said I could never be honest with you because
what I had to say would make you mad.
You then got mad and didn't speak to me
for months. Before you shut the door, your last
wounding words were these: *I've told people
all my life what an angel you are.
Now I have to tell them you're a bitch.*

The months stretched on without a word, honest
or no. I bought a ticket on the Greyhound,
traveled a thousand worried miles to see
you in your stucco house with its giant
pink mimosa tree. I limped through the door,
the bandage on my foot spotted with blood.
What's happened? you cried. *It won't heal,* I said.

I stepped on a stick, and now the wound's infected.
You replied, *Sit down.* From the kitchen,
you fetched Epsom salts, a pan of water,
fresh white gauze, a tube of antiseptic.
Bending down, just as you must have done
to tie my shoe, you washed my festering foot
in silence. It didn't matter I wasn't an angel,
It didn't matter we had no words to say.

My Daughter Is Transfigured

Mother, you said you were tired
of putting yourself together every
morning inhaling expensive drugs
to loosen the drawstrings of your lungs.
I tell you it has taken
all these interim years of living
to put together words telling
what I saw five days after
you breathed your last on your knees,
grasping at that thinning strand
of what is understood as life,
three days after you were laid
to rest, to see the mystery
of the inextricable
fluidity of being, whether
newly born or newly dead
when the sleeping form of my
twenty-year-old daughter was lying
beside me under double quilts,
both of us needing not
to be alone that winter night.
Lost to myself, as wrenching grief
will do, light weakly streaming
from the kitchen door ajar,
I looked at my daughter's face
then looked again, puzzled to see
not her face but yours, Mother,
not her fine-boned youthful visage
but your high dramatic cheekbones
your skin thin translucent pale
and your hair, your long black hair,
pinned up in a pompadour.
Not frightened, curious as I traced
your features transposed upon her face,
and, with an intake of my breath,
understood that she was mother.

Wedding Picture
    for Thatcher Michael Kimball (1981-2013)

Your sister
who had once brought you
underwear and a toothbrush

to the restricted hospital ward
who had given you a home with her
who, on this day, had ordered a meal for you

to eat alone, at the celebration—
she did not know
that on this, her wedding day

would be the last half hug she'd receive
from your nearly weightless arms.
Your brother had sent a suit,

which you had purchased a tie for,
and unsuitable shoes for.
You left your ailing cat,

driving five hundred desert miles
in a rusting truck
setting your jaw firm to face

the crowd of guests and revelers.
After the wedding, after the photos,
after the dinner and the dancing

which you left us to,
you left us. What time
did you pack up that morning

and drive away
in your black pick-up
putting desert miles between us?

This is the last picture
we have of you
handsome, brave

distant in your grey suit
standing in silence
life locked away

although the desert
is laden with bloom
and all the girls are wearing blue.

A Tale

The very best part was holding her in her room of painted birds:

Lilsie and I in the summer dark, she snuffling while I rocked,
her breath catching on raspy edges,

and all around, the familiars of nestling—
soft bed, ragged bunny

the rustling of the shade
the slowing creak of oaken bands beneath us.

Our Happiness
after Eileen Myles

was when we
found a hotel
for fifty francs
a night
sheets drying on the banister

we stored milk on the window ledge
warmed soup on a burner
the whole city lit
outside the window

later we stayed
in a friend's
apt. on the seventh floor
where there was a small
stove & we could make
love without crude drawings
being slipped under our door

we took turns bathing
in the square tub in the kitchen
using the same lukewarm water

you were music-starved &
we found
a record player
in the closet

one day in the
late afternoon
we consumed
Rachmaninoff's Concerto #2
the whole city lit
on the unmade bed

Love Poem for My Husband
February 19, 2017

There is a felt presence.
The drooping cups of snowdrops
stiffen on their stalks,
water ices over

in the sludgy pond,
and the sun hides
like a dropped quarter
behind a cushion
of morning grey.

He sits cross-legged
in the room's winter light,
his anxious mind

seeking a clearing of thought,
a letting go,
a quiet dismissal
of the past.

Now he rises, hopeful
that this, another day
of bitter wind
yet might bring to him

contentment:
there is space
again, the beech hedge
quivering its brown leaves,

and there is love,
the mossy trees
and stones constant
in their being.

Jung Potatoes

After years of thin soup,
I'm cooking up poems *de terre* these days,
learning how to slow boil.

So I wasn't surprised when
my long neglected *animus*
appeared one night, starched
and ready for action,
in a chef's crisp jacket.

I'm busy making my dream potatoes,
folding in the dream butter, the dream cream,
when he appears, gorgeous,
and, may I add, très *appétissant*,
in a sexy Parisian kind of way,

although I can't help but notice
a dark crusty speck
on his starched white coat.

Maybe I'm transgressing kitchen rules,
but I can't help myself.
I, with timid pleasure,
reach up to
unspot his smock.

An intimacy well-met—
because his hand seizes mine—
and then from those sensual Gallic lips —
a declaration of wild and reckless love.

By all dream rights
now is the time to wrench off the eight buttons
from his high-quality, cotton twill chef's attire,

send them sailing in all directions,
over the six-sealed gas-burner range,
behind the thirty-four cubic foot
high capacity French refrigerator.

Now is the moment
to sing out, "yes, yes, yes!
O, mon chou, mon cher lapin!"
to make delicious, well-seasoned love,
on the expanse of the yellow rubberwood butcher block top,
so ideal for prep tasks and serving,
to gasp, sputter, spill love and more love
down to a last soufflé—
which, in a dream kitchen,
one has every right to expect.

But no.
I tell him
no.
I say, in the plainest dream language I can muster,
my life is complicated.

Then, I wake,
madly in love—
but mad, in fact,
full of animus, in fact,
because
it's just like me to refuse,
because, and I'm speaking to you,
my ambitious *animus*,
and telling you something you already know:

your other half is a thwarted spinster of verse
who has kept us both far too long
on a diet of cold potatoes.

I Thought I Knew It All

I knew it all. I had landed in a cotton field and had become a boll—cotton for eyes, ears, mouth, a state of exquisite materialism.

My friend knew nothing. "Know nothing; trust everyone" was his motto, even after his accountant absconded to Switzerland with every pence of his Heritage grant, awarded to restore his beloved medieval ruin. So, it remained a ruin. He cheerfully propped up a crumbling wing—and for thirty years lived roofless, keeping the grass in manicured order. He wrote a long letter to my new address, speaking of his rubble as he would a lover: "You must see her in May; she's in her glory!"

Meanwhile, my cotton eyes were closed. I knew everything and trusted no one. I was safe inside my capsule, protected with four thorn-like claws. Think of it! I could hear no one and no one could hear me. In any case, I couldn't say much, maybe "owfowfowf." That was sufficient until the cotton pickers came, tore me out of my soft existence, stripped me of my seeds, left me for the balers. I was on my way to a new existence but hovered above my friend's roofless pile long enough to shout down, "I knowfnowfing!"

A Blessing
after James Wright

In suburban Maplewood,
Late afternoon sun pools on a white carpet,
And my old grey cat, foundling, one eye blind,
Leaps from the bed.
She has interrupted her nap
To study me on the floor, crying.
She circles once,
And I raise my head to see her
Padding. She turns her good eye towards me
To see what is afoot in this human world.
She's skittish as a sparrow.
There's no cat heart like hers.
On alert, she stalks the prey-like object
Of my sadness.
I would like to take her in my arms,
But such display never suited.
She stays close.
Grey and small,
Each foot furred in white
Prim as Sunday shoes.
As I bend once more to my grief,
She sidles closer.
Suddenly I feel
Her scratchy pink tongue
Licking my arm again and again
Giving her kind of compassion.

West Seventy-Sixth St.

she was old
in human years ninety-six
she had never lost
her grace

she was petite had a grey coat
often matted and spotted with dandruff
& though she hated the vet's
grooming she felt better for the visit

she resisted the carrier
but once inside she submitted
to the inevitable—rode the subway
to West Seventy-Sixth in stoic silence

let me say she wasn't my cat
she was a hand-me-down
a charge that I resisted—
just like my teenager—

to leave me with this responsibility
he had found her in a shrub
crying abandoned the runt of
the litter he wrapped her in his jacket

& brought her home
the vet said feed her
meat strained for babies
have her spayed at first opportunity

I agreed a reluctant yes because
it was a comfort to me
this show of tenderness for the world
from a lonely son who would leave soon

for darker days
that was twenty years ago
now he is gone
one day I will tell of his going

this poem tells of his stray
who ate and drank
her little rations
up until the last day

who never missed the litter box
who could still leap high into her chair
& never passed a human leg
without waiting for a nuzzle

a toe under her delicate fine-boned
neck softly white
was all she asked for
when I found her stretched

out on her bony side
on the bathroom tiled floor
a thin thread of blood from her nose
blood crusts on her immaculate paws

I wrapped her in a towel
rocked her like the baby
I once had told her she had been
a good kitty

she barely stirred—I laid her down
beside me & called the vet
when she passes bring her in
which consoled to have someone

with me an animal's death
is not so different from our own
glazed eyes—I could see
no rise of fur from the still form

brought in the carrier undid
the metal clasps—startlingly—
she raised her head thought I
was in too much of a hurry

she was not going to the vet
I lay down beside her
all night I lay down beside her
in the morning her form hardened

into a statue's only then
did I wrap her—place her
into the carrier & take her
to West Seventy-Sixth St.

&

& did you know that the ampersand
is derived from the ligature of et,
Latin for *and*?

& did you know that until 1837
the ampersand was considered the 27th letter
of the alphabet?

& though it wasn't a letter,
"... XYZ and *per se* and"—
that's what school children recited.

& do you think you have an overfill
of such trivia?
& will you howl to add another bit?

& you may not know this, but
the brain's axons and dendrites
stretched end to end would be 500,000 miles long.

& that's the way I feel about my life—
500,000 miles long now, enough memory
to go around the earth twenty times.

&&&&&&&&&&&&&&&c

Palimpsest
Sappho's fragments indicated by brackets

You left me—a[nd this overhan]ging
des[tructive spirit] now pressing down on me
means that I [truly did not lik]e seeing your old red dress
hanging in the closet; [now because] I go and look at it daily,
hanging there in the closet—[the cause neither] I nor the gods can discern
for this absurdity— I am left wondering why
this threadbare scrap could possibly matter
when [nothing much] else has cost me tears.

Crossings
>*for Morris Arrari (1949-2008)*

I.
The sleep of this night is broken
because I have heard my name called
and have crossed the hall into the sickroom
carrying crushed ice in a white cup.
All night it will offer thin drink
from its paper lip to his.

Under weak light, I watch
his breath rise and fall.
Tonight, his last night, he wants to talk.
I make space on the dark bed,
we two, stretched out together,
on the worn quilt.

II.
On a hot day in Salonika, 1951,
your father has finished his thick coffee.
Your mother has laid out a white shirt,
its sleeves long to cover
the black numbers tattooed
above his wrist. The bags are packed.

Now, while the transatlantic steamer waits
in the shade of the White Tower,
you, a small boy, run along the quay,
your arms open to embrace your life,
not your father's,
but one requiring his strength.

III.
We remember this,
and our own expectant youth,
when the ocean was crossed once more,
our meeting on the liner to Elysium,
both having irreverent songs to sing
on upturned Parisian cobbles
then, as now, in a dream.

Rest in my arms, dear friend,
your head against my old grey sweater.
Before another ocean is crossed,
we'll remember the words
to that old song of grace,
then we'll be quiet.

The Simple Heart of Things

> ... *le cœur simple*
> *triomphe dans l'éclat*
> *et la transparence de la lumière.*
> —Guy Goffette, from "*L'ordalie*"

... the simple heart
triumphs in the brilliance
and transparency of light.

And when it was my turn
to sit at the bedside
of our dying friend
there was beauty there.

I learned what I did not know:
death does not always mean terror.
As he descended further and further
into the mystery, he folded like the lotus.

Near the end of his passage,
he could not speak;
he could only hear—his only sense
a full singing bowl of sound.

I finished one life and
found another;
and though the light wavers
bright, then fades,

I can almost say
that the end
seems to me
a golden turning.

A Dream

In a grassy field of bluebells
which stretched along a mile
I sat upon a lichened stone
to rest a little while.

Then I laid my body down
and cried out years of pain
until the burdens in my heart
dissolved in gentle rain.

I fell asleep and dreamed a dream
I'll treasure till I die
that in this grassy field of bluebells
the two of us did lie.

Leaves Falling in Late October
for Tu Fu, 8th c. Chinese poet

Congratulations, leaves,
you know when to fall

coming down at all hours
taking a stroll in the wind

making a shower of color
on dirty streets

brightening dull pavement
for my neighbors

the old feel blessed
when they walk out for a ramble

I stand at the window
thinking nothing much is worth attaching to

you hold on as long as you can
then make a beauty of your passing

Kathryn Kimball has a Ph.D. in English Literature and an MFA in Poetry and Poetry in Translation. From 1991—2007, she taught writing and nineteenth-century British and American literature as an adjunct professor at Drew University. Her translations and poems have appeared in *Transference, The Galway Review,* and elsewhere.

She grew up in Montgomery, Alabama, attended college in the West, and raised a family of six in the Northeast. Her crossings now span the U.S. and the Atlantic. She spends several months of every year in a cottage in the north of England, in Cumbria, near the Scottish border.

A practitioner of yoga for twenty-five years, she lives with her husband in New York City.

www.ingramcontent.com/pod-product-compliance
Lightning Source LLC
LaVergne TN
LVHW041600070426
835507LV00011B/1209